PRIVATE RYAN

PRIVATE RYAN
Volume I

A Collection of Poems and Micro Poetry
By Ryan Baird

Dedication

This is to the Sharon's in my life.

First and foremost, my little sister Sharon Church,
for always being a known constant throughout my life.

Then there's Sharon Baldock, a wonderful friend
and fellow connoisseur of playful shenanigans

Lastly and by no means least there's Sharon Johnson.
Without her there wouldn't be this book. For her
encouragement I will be forever grateful.

Contents

Preface 11

Love & Lust

The Poets Touch 15
Halo 17
Closer 19
Confusion 21
Love and Lost 23
Lurking Vision 25
True 27
Share 29
Separate 31
Touché 33
Drifting 35
Desire 37
Senses 39

Depression

Facades 43
Pain 45
Changes 47
Future 49
Curious 51
Splinted 53

Heartbreak

Blades	57
Three of Hearts	59
The last stand	61
Spoken	63
Probable	65
Scream	67
Freedom Lost	69

Hope

Tides	73
Smother	75
Mate	77
Vision	79
Wait	81

Anger

Myriad	85
Blood in/Blood out	87
The End	89
Damned	91

Family

Beginnings	95
Bonds	97
Coming of age	99
Age	101
Grace	103

Questions

- Balance 107
- Pathways 109
- Dreamscape 111
- Haunted 113
- Freedom 115
- Searching 117

Friendship

- One 121
- Acknowledgment 123
- The gift 125
- Shard 127
- The shack 129
- Flight 131

Micro Poetry

- Depression-Despondency-Melancholy 135
- Dominance-Submission-Sin 137
- Friendship-Devotion-Solidarity 139
- Happiness-Joy-Rapture 141
- Love-Passion-Lust 143
- Musing-Inspirational-Random 145
- Sadness-Loss-Grief 147
- Wrath-Anger-Rage 149

About The Author

- Ryan Baird 151

Preface

This is a book 20 years in the making. The poems were written during chaotic times of my youth. Adrift and aimless I tried to find answers to questions I couldn't find and didn't have the courage to ask.

Trying to find any kind of clarity while transitioning from budding adolescence to manhood was difficult and my scattered emotions were a measure of this.

The content of this book was written during this time. The exceptions being The Poets Touch at the start of he book and the micro poetry found towards the back of the book.

Reading these poems after so long I realise just how far I have travelled along life's path and how this has affected the evolution of my writing.

I have held onto these poems for so long but as a part of the creative journey it's time to let go of the past, move into the present and plan for the future.

As terrifying it is to show the inner workings of my often scattered mind and somewhat tortured soul it's time to let the world see what I have kept hidden for so long and it's hoped somewhere along the line someone will take some measure of inspiration from my written word.

Love & Lust

The Poets Touch

A poets muse lies in his lovers touch
Words written with gentle caresses on willing flesh
Every moan, every sigh lines for his poetry
The radiance of her soul his light in which he writes
He holds her close to his tortured heart
Cherished and sacred, her spirit beckons
Once more his hands seek his inspiration
Shadowed movements provoking trembling cries
The lover's imagination defining pleasured craving
Sought for release found as she comes undone
The poet in a moment clarity writes true
His lover, his muse, his one and his only….

Halo

I have wept crimson
Sated my anger
Broken ties to indifference
All that is left is us
A future best left uncertain
For the present is ours
We have shared many things you and I
Thoughts, passion and trust
I trust you with much more than I can give
Given openly and only to you
For it is you that I wish to give unto
A gift from within our dreams
We have shared the dreaming moment
Wished for that immortal day
That inner radiance, the true you
The purity of a moment left untainted
One perfect day
One stolen kiss
Locked within my mind
Unchained by my heart
And given with my soul....

Closer

Movements
Movements that seek to enthral me
Thought provoking and erotic
Preluding whispers of things to come
Longing looks and passionate embraces
Kissing, feeling, probing
Seeking more heat, more desire
Intimacy being the key to unlocking known joy
The key to passion, the key to love
Use that key to unlock your feelings
Release all that you hold within you
And you will be free....

Confusion

Confusion for a woman
Confusion for riotous thoughts running rampant
I know all about this woman, yet I know nothing
I don't know how or what I feel
Do I love her? Do I know what love is?
There is no denying the attraction
It binds us and draws us together
How will I know that my feelings are shared?
I will wait, wait for her and watch
Watching to see our potential love blossom
As we come full circle
The two of us coming together
Completing love's cycle....

Love and Lost

How can something seem so right yet seem so wrong
I can't deny my feelings, my swelling emotions
Why must I deny these burgeoning feelings?
It's because of the friendship of another that I hold back
On that night, that first night that we met
I gazed upon your beauty, so strong, yet fragile
Thinking that if I were to blink you would disappear
You are to me like water passing through my fingers
Knowing I could never hold you for long or contain you
This expresses what I cannot say without clarity
It shows what I feel and what I feel is you....

Lurking Vision

What power lurks behind our eyes?
What makes them bewitch, bewilder and infuriate?
If you or I were to look into those eyes
Those bright and beautiful eyes
You can see what a person is thinking or feeling
Within others I have seen anger unchained
Found confusion, sought lust and known affection
All this pales to finding love unmasked....

True

A friend
A very special friend
Special in the way we talk
The way we act in the others presence
It is because of our friendship
That I won't tell her how I feel
How do I feel you ask?
I love her
Plainly, passionately and intimately
I can't tell you how much
Or how deep these feelings run
She is everything I ever wanted in a woman
Kind, intense, beautiful
She is strong where others were weak
We talk on so many levels that defy description
She excites and stirs feelings that I never knew I had
Or ever felt before
I will stay away from her
For she may find out how I feel
How she'll react I don't know
Don't look…..

Share

The definition, a kiss
Crudely begun with passion
Forged with heart
Tempered by soul
The hunger for the present
Wishing for times flowing grace past
Drifting to where we both belong
Twisting, moving, expanding
Sharing this great symphony that we call our hearts
Beating hard, beating fast
The breath hot against our faces
Held together by a focus
Our cherished sanctuary
Can't be touched, can't be heard
Memory shared
My lips meet yours
The defining moment
The kiss….

Separate

Sleeping single, sleeping alone
Quiet nights spent in painful separation
The loss of your warmth
And the feeling of your contented heart
Beating hard, beating together
A union makes us as one
As we fall into one another
The memory of which makes me whole
You have given to me a feeling I thought lost
That lucid feeling of safety within a woman's embrace
Will you give yourself to me?
Will I give myself to you?
Can we find happiness in the future?
A future spent in dreaming moments
Moments, days, nights
You have time
I hope you have patience....

Touché

Beginnings
The feelings of complacency
Searching for hard truths
Where I look for equality
To have love expand
To find security in the warmth of our union
To breathe in and taste the essence of you
Heat rising and increasing by passions joy
Feel the strength, savour the moment
Time passes
Leaving us falling into one another
Trembling without and within
Drifting to the place that can't be touched
If not by us then by no-one
This is more than physical pleasure
It is a touching of souls
A love, a good love
Good and strong
It is our love....

Drifting

Two worlds colliding
Form to create a union
This union creates trust
Unrelenting passions
Unspeakable secrets
As I lay my life before you
As you did for me
I have come to love your shine
Your inner beauty
Seen through my eyes
Friendship so close it hurts
Relationship so indefinable
It causes me confusion as it does you
I now understand you
Your pains and agonies
It is this knowledge that allows me to do this
It was this knowledge that helped me to let go
Of you, of me….

Desire

If regret was to be
With memories of anger and discontent
All bring about the madness of the moment
The moment burning with the desire to belong
The need to love as passion begins to surge
Blazing white hot with the throb of my heart
The beat, the pulse, the rhythm divine
It beats for one
 My perfect ideal beautiful woman born of purity
Sought and desired by one, this imperfect, flawed beast
Trying so hard to contain the revenants of his past
The past which destroys all
Hoping for the freedom of the future
As we soar into oblivion together
Entwined in the sanctity of a life together….

Senses

A whispered sweet moment
A vision of delicate beauty
An elaborate symphony
One essential friend
The black eternity of raw light
A shadow of a summer rose
The woman I recall
Time, dreams
Shine from you
My love....

Depression

Facades

I am alone once again
Emotions and energy surge throughout my body
Contemplating feelings of love and lust
Only to find it unrequited
Feelings of anger, need to lash out
At what? As I find myself raging
I need a sign, a focus, a welcome distraction
I question what is it that I'm scared of?
Love lived, love received and love denied
Who will stand through with me through this?
I must be strong during complicated doubt
Maintain the mask, present the façade
Drawing into myself I find myself lost
Confusion all around, as once again I'm alone
Always alone….

Pain

Looking into my soul I find pain and suffering
Ripping into me with an animalistic fury
Fragmenting my soul, my feelings and my emotions
Feelings of neglect, as I split into shadows
I try to hide within myself but get caught, trapped
Contained by the one thing I can't escape; myself….

Changes

Help me
I have become bogged down in a fit of self-loathing
As I unwillingly drag others into my personal hell
They see the dark half of my soul, naked for them to see
They say I've changed and this is true I have
I've lost my innocence or whatever
innocence I may have had
The change occurring form within,
so sudden it scares others
Where is the loving, caring and
happy man they once knew?
You'll find him buried deep within the
darkest depths of my subconscious
He may be hiding but the change has still occurred
Irreversible, unstoppable, live with it
Without a choice I have....

Future

I have come to a crossroads
Where I go now I do not know
This is the borderline of love and hate
Light or dark, peace or war
Do I go left and right or up and down?
Which way will bring peace or oblivion?
Contradictions confuse with vertigo pushing
My world, my life thrown into chaos
Spreading me out, drawing me out
Draining me and sapping my will
I take the first step, not caring where I'm going
Out of sight, out of mind….

Curious

Questions
What is it that you want to know?
What is it that you are too scared to ask?
I know you want answers but I need the questions
Will you ask them?
Or are you scared I may tell you my truth?
You know me, but constantly seek more
What do you need to know?
How far will you delve?
How much do you want?
If I reveal myself
My soul naked for you to see
How will you react?
You want to know
Apprehension holds you back
Curiosity pushes you
More or less, ripped and torn
Light and dark
Close to what we fear
The shadows, watch the shadows
Feel my pain become manifest
Accept it, accept me....

Splinted

What do you see? What do I feel?
This I ask to my dancing shadows
Cold, this mind numbing sense of dejection
So wretched I feel sick and alone
I have friends but none I can talk to
The next level, I dwell there alone
People try to reach me upon this vista
Selfishly I spurn them all
Why?
Because I don't want them to see me
See us, two minds, one soul
You can't reach what I can't touch
Talk to me if you can find me….

Heartbreak

Blades

Mental or physical pain, which hurts more?
Physical pain will heal in time
Mentally you may never heal
Leaving this body shattered and this mind broken
With nothing left to show but a
few bittersweet memories
Promised empty words of things to come
Hollow words coming from someone
I have only glimpsed upon
Opening myself up to her, has left me vulnerable
A tortured puppet for her to toy with
Simply rejecting me would've worked
but she cut me, cut me deep
She then proceeded to twist her pseudo knife deeper
The knife still remains; she may or may not know
That only she can remove the blade
To remove the blade or push deeper
To live or to die, this is her choice
My life is in her hands….

Three of Hearts

Once more I have done what could've been avoided
I have done what could've been denied
The denial being a lie and I won't lie
For when I lie I lie to myself as well as her
Finding unresolved feeling for another
Must I fragment? So as to incorporate the other
No: I must choose
For while I love one I lust after the other
Love or lust, which will prove to be the greater emotion?
The confusion may see me lose both
I will make the choice and I only pray it's the right one
That it will be only time will tell....

The last stand

A kiss is just a kiss; a touch is just a touch
Leaving only hollow words and hollow promises
Whispered words that will remain unspoken
Words that need to be communicated
Sparing and avoiding possible confusion
Where to stand as you have felt my heart
The cadence of my heartbeat beneath my chest
Memories come unbidden of softly spoken words
Lingering touches and what is now last caresses
There is no need for such confusing
and bittersweet memories
Maybe I should hate the person who caused such pain
This I cannot do and why I do not know
I don't even know if what remains is friendship
Friends who have seen the good and
bad of each other's soul
I don't know if it makes us closer, probably not
I will never know the truth of questions unanswered….

Spoken

Words
I see none, I hear none
Why are they not spoken?
What is left to be said?
Said to who and for what
We will be silent
In this silence we die
Not in body, but in soul
Depriving us of what we need most
Say it! And yet you still wait
Because you fear the confrontation
Why?
Denied....

Probable

I lied, but once
A stolen moment
Moments, time, space
All mean the same to me
I felt more, I know less
I spoke to you, you spoke to me
Lacking proven understanding
Creating greater confusion
Rough thoughts with jagged edges
Immature and inexperienced
Body and mind
Age and life
Kindred spirits
Look up and I will look down
Down at you, as you rise
Touché
Impossible…..

Scream

A moment in time
A singular experience
Silence and isolation
Forged by iron of my own making
Deeply cut by a shattered heart
Fragmented into useless shards
A soul exorcised by unwanted yearnings
The pure spirit not yet tainted
Tied to a shell of past pain
Responsible for none
Responsible for all
Redemption wasted on a fool
Slipping away, slipping away
Help not given strength
As everything turns crimson
Lost with agonizing failure
I lost, I let go
I fell from grace
My silent prison
My bittersweet tears….

Freedom Lost

Azure dreams cloud my vision
Sight lost on a broken view
Ripped apart by fragmented ego
Corruption bleeds throughout my core
A self-destructive push towards oblivion
The yearning abyss staring and
Struggling for release
A release that will not come
Beckoning from within
Fragments of agonized yearnings
How true to the cause, how straight to the quick
A seized moment to reflect upon the crazed journey
The journey where control must be
abhorred by all along the path
Compartments bulging with raw strength from chaos
Focus found with the northern light
Martyred saints dwell in the shadows of indecision
I made my choice and have accepted my role in the game
Choices; Roles; Games; Obligations
The clipped wings, the azure dream….

Hope

Tides

I have come to this place
My most secret place
A haven, a place for escapes
This place complicated for some
But primal for others
No one but I know of this place
It is beyond the break and across the sea
Will you come with me?
Come embrace the safety of my sanctuary
Come feel the breeze flow through your hair
Feel the salt water at your feet
Come, come join me
Let us drift away together....

Smother

Darkness
Enveloping me in its embrace
Smothering me and crushing my faith
Drilling into me and filling me
Covering every contour of my body
Can't hide from pervasive shadows
Darkness everywhere
Where is the light and who is the light?
Reaching out I find it
In the deep recesses of my turbulent mind
Focusing I gain insight as I open my eyes
And there was light…..

Mate

I need you as you need me
We have lived for each other
Existence diminished without one another
I look to you for strength for I have no more
You will fight my demons as I have fought yours
I won the battle but the war has been lost
Lost to me and given to you
We will fight together
In the face of hardship, pain
We face it together
The two of us, as we walk into oblivion….

Vision

Contention
You want to enter the race
But are held back by doubts
Why is this so?
You have defined naivety
Is that such a crime?
You are young, inexperienced
You need to grow
Visualize your life as you age
Within today's society where not much is sacred
You have retained a spark of purity
Both in body and soul
I see both burning brightly
It is said that beauty is in the eyes of the beholder
Physical beauty is purely cosmetic
What counts is your inner beauty
Beauty that comes from the heart and soul
Wake up to life and enjoy
Complacent you sit back
In faith and in patient hope I found in you
This belief I hold close and I give it to you....

Wait

I said goodbye
But goodbyes aren't forever
As you and I know
I wait with baited breath for your return
To once more be with you
To laugh with, to cry with
Many special moments spent together
Moments shared
Through good times and bad times
I was there
For when you return
I will still be there
Waiting....

Anger

Myriad

What lies between my eyes?
I look to quell my raging passions
Passions that drive me onward
Needing to hide these feelings
I create a mask to hide my fiery emotions
A façade broken and undone by my eyes
Eyes that if you know how to read them
You will unlock the key to my withheld emotions
Emotions that, if left unchecked will rage out of control
With this I ask what it is you see within my eyes
For when look within my eyes you
will see and feel many things
You will be very amused, happy or relaxed
Or you will be very, very scared
For when you look into my eyes
You will see the good within me
Or the inherit evil that lurks within….

Blood in/Blood out

What has happened?
You walk away and I will not follow
Talk to me, no longer
Ignoring me, is a silent risk
Look away and you will lose
I am raging against betrayal
Disrespected with lost affection
Links broken, hearts separated
Dreams no longer shared
Shattered, as shadows lengthen
My oblivion, drowning in anger
I will walk into it the darkness alone
Without you, without me
Why are you doing this?
What has happened?....

The End

Brothers no more
Comrades no more
No more you, no more us
A confidence kept by me
One you couldn't keep
Damn you, I trusted you
My secrets, my life, my soul
You did this and yes it was funny
This dark humour was not lost on me
Laugh, go on, laugh at me
I was blind, blind to you
Naïvely I believed in you
When others did not
Betrayed by you
Traitor, back off
Unforgiven….

Damned

My heart beats like a drum
God help me
My blood burns like fire in my veins
As I prepare to sin
My muscles tense
A coming conflict
A need to be ready
I bleed freely and readily
The blood of a maniac
As I run through the land
Searching for prey
Prey and redemption
More blood is spilt
Not mine, the victim
As I bite deeper
Devouring her whole, her essence
Cleansed, my sins have gone
Washed away in a baptism of blood
Laughing at death I continue the hunt
Death you can't touch me
Because I don't fear you….

Family

Beginnings

Two people share a moment
The most intimate of moments
The moment isn't just shared by these two
It's is shared with another
The other that was conceived through their union
This union brought forth a life
Created through the miracle of love
It was this love that created this life
This life was their son
Although this love has now soured
I remain as a testament to their love
Their lost love
Caught within the two I fragment
Holding tight to my love for them
I draw them close and closer to my heart
It was this love that allowed me to find myself again
Love for my dad and love for my mum....

Bonds

What is it that bonds us?
Is it love? Is it trust?
No, it is neither
It is knowing
Knowing the other's feeling
Knowing the other's thinking
Feeling the others thoughts
Feeling the empathy between us
Memories of times had and times lost
Just thinking of these memories brings
about a myriad of emotions
Happiness, contentment, affection, love
All this and more I get from thinking
of times had together
The warm feeling that I get from the pit of my stomach
Rises from within to bring a bright smile to my face
This is what you must do
For whenever you are alone, sad or depressed
Just seek me out and I will be there
To laugh with you, to cry with you
I would do all of this and more not
because I'm your brother
But because I'm your best friend
And you are my sister….

Coming of age

I have seen the child within the woman
I know the child well
For the child is a part of me
Her innocence is stolen from her
As well as her happiness
Hurting me as it hurts her
I feel her pain as she feels mine
She comes to me for release, comfort
Cradling her in my arms I accept her pain
Acting as a barrier for her hurt
My strong arms protecting her
The two entities lost without each other
Form to become a whole
The union forms knowledge
Knowledge of unbreakable love and trust
She knows of my loyalty to her happiness
And heaven help anyone that dares take it from her
So if you ask if I know of the child within the woman
The woman within the child then
my answer would be yes
For the child is sister
The child has become a woman
And for this I'm happy….

Age

How do you measure age?
Be it years? I think not
I think age is a representative of life
Experiences form a basis of maturity
In turn creating personality
And putting all together you have wisdom
You may not be the wisest
But then again neither am I
Though I do know what I feel in my heart
And what I see with my mind
Age has formed what you are today
No longer a child, but a woman
A woman with ideals and dreams of her own
Dreams that we share
That I share with my sister
My baby sister
You know as I do
Just how difficult it is to say this
But I do care and love you
In a way many may not understand
But we do....

Grace

God is the name given to mothers
on the lips of their children
My mother may not be a god but to
me she is an amazing person
Her stubborn, steadfast views may
be difficult to deal with
But these same views have held her in good stead
Allowing her to rise above the rest
Her single-minded determination stands
as an example to those that may fall
That no matter what will happen or how
much time it may take to get there
It won't just be determination that will get her there
But also a lot of pride and perseverance
Life may have dealt out a lot of pain
But rather than give in it has made her stronger
This strength is what bonds me to her
For I respect and love her for it
This love gives me the strength to go on
As we walk into the future together….

Questions

Balance

Without balance the centre won't hold
Without a centre you have no focus
Focus without life, life without focus
Sins to be cleansed, deeds to be praised
Washed in a pool of life blood
The blood of me, the blood of you
The blood of the innocent
Washed clear until white becomes red
Collective minds, the fragile web
Tread carefully
For it may be strong
But it will not hold you....

Pathways

The angels look and laugh
Misgivings? I have none
All because I was true
Truths known as emotions swell
Hacking and slashing randomly
Ripping and tearing savagely
Raging resentment and painfully curious
I have few answers but many questions
Look as I weep crimson
Fiery red for the passion
Am I not in control of my kingdom?
Who I am? I take comfort in not knowing
Beauty, within and without
As with the rose
Beauty known amongst this crown of thorns
However if you're not careful you'll get hurt
A hard and difficult lesson….

Dreamscape

The prize
Coveted by many and given to one
A revenant of past passions
Unfelt within the delirium
Silent Morpheus claims his prize
The gateway hidden, truth to be found
I saw what I most covet
Transformed within the circle
Caught within his grasp
I see, I feel, I taste this forbidden fruit
Stolen from the Garden of Eden
The face I have grown to love
Changed to leave me alone
The need to have, own, belong
Bludgeoning me with monotony
To be within but not without
The taste I won't soon forget
But I have already forgotten
A betrayal known only to me
Burns me from within
A passionate pause
Take control, come to me….

Haunted

The pains from the past present me with the hatred
Lost hope in the present gave me love in the future
An uncomfortable feeling to be complete
The first time in an age
Animalistic urges as darkness rises
Compelled to give into my shadow
How I long to be free from my cage
Silence spent in tearful mourning
Convert, converse and automate
The game spent
My strength, my body, my soul
Hard as it must be, for the rules will change
As will I, this is my life, my world
To myself will control be given?
A dreaming moment
Dawning horizons
My silent prayers….

Freedom

To be jealous of a thought
A confused trial of error
Too many moments spent in quiet contemplation
The sorrow felt with harsh inadequacies
Innuendo not touched upon in the confusion
Stylish metaphors mixed with bitter tears
Used together to savour the truth
A different perspective of all
Vast intelligence and wisdom complete both
Experience and age overshadow unions
Time frame and the moment not taken
Pressure built up by degrees
My fever, the desire to be
The eyes, fiery red betray all
Passion, lust, want and love
Also seeing the person as a thing of beauty
To grant hands to mould and craft
Biased as my view but it is mine
To look without conscious
To touch without fear
To love without regrets
It is a dream I have…..

Searching

I have struggled through so much
Fought through death, setbacks and crisis
Reaching out for that distant and dimming light
To grasp that which continually eludes me
That wondrously benevolent feeling; love
What is it? How do you define it?
I have seen glimpses of it through my eyes or others
Is it passion? Is it compromise? Is it affection?
It is all these things and more
It is loving someone more than yourself
Love is unselfishly giving more than you receive
To love someone for what they are
Not what you would want them to be
All I have given, strength, time, essence
Lost, for I cannot grasp the intimacy
The intimacy of being without
Why keep trying you ask?
It is the strength of the human spirit, my spirit
One more setback, one more headache
Strength, age, maturity, I go on
A dangerous game
An incredibly beautiful prize….

Friendship

One

To be with one
Past revenants to be forgotten
As I look to the future, our future
Pains to be cleansed, as we heal
And as we heal so will we grow
For the healing heralds new experiences
Passionately passive yet patiently controlled
Thank you, as when you helped me
So we will begin to help each other
A new day, an indifferent era
The past is dead
The future is now....

Acknowledgment

The pathway taken
The road less travelled
The connection found
You saw what others did not
Saw past the mask
The smile hiding grievous pains
Unrelenting and unselfishly poised
By me, with me and beside me
You, it was you
You felt my ripped soul and my torn heart
Care nurtured me and your friendship strengthened me
I will be there for you as you were for me
A moment; past? Will it rest?
Time used in idiotic masquerades
Another time, another place
A perfect world…..

The gift

A refreshing change
The change from the taking
For it was you who gave
Given to me to safeguard
A secret given to few
And known by less
So in exchange a gift
My gift to you has many shapes
It is merely how you perceive it
For it can give you many things
As all that I can give I will
The beauty that is you
Is the light which pierces my night
It is this light which guides me
Guides me to you
To your trust, to your friendship
Friendship I can give
Trust we can work on
I'm sure we have time….

Shard

A present from one friend to another
A gift that can't be borrowed, stolen or lent
It must be given
Coming from my heart
I give the gift freely
And in doing so I give a part of myself
In return I ask for nothing
For you have already bestowed the greatest gift of all
Your friendship....

The shack

No pressure
A call taken up by all that lay within
The phrase has become the institution
The institution has become a way of life
It is this life that brings us to this place
A place for escapes
A place for friends
A place for fun
To others it may not seem like much
But to us it's paradise, a paradise where;
Anything can done
Anything is possible
A place where's life's problems can be forgotten
And if there was to be a problem
Everyone would call out in unison
No pressure….

Flight

A friendship defined in ruptured lines
Musings on damaged ideals
A silent whisper to closed secrets
Our knowledge shared alone and within
My strength lifting and with purpose
Your radiant grace, shuttered
Closed and fragmented as I try to capture light
Mapping the corridors of this endless maze
We run, we laugh, we share, we play
The game based on loose provocation
Rules of which we know all too well
To understand that which I never will
Peace found in moments
A priceless gift
Your smile, my friend
Thank you....

Micro Poetry

Depression-Despondency-Melancholy

Conducting Pain

If hopes were dreams my hope, my wish would
be to act as a conduit for your pain….

Caged Clarity

The caged Angel
Imprisoned for no crime
Freedom sought from indecision
Chains destroyed when clarity is found….

Small Denial

Even the smallest of my demons seek to deny me rest
Insomnia seeks to take sleep from me yet again….

Lonely Company

Forever surrounded & always alone
There is no greater sorrow than
the loneliness of company
Not felt within or without….

Lost and Denied

The mind his greatest prison
Solid bars of his own design
Unbreakable & impenetrable he remains
The key, his freedom
Lost and denied....

My Gift

To summon pain from memory
Heartache from painful separations
This is my gift, unwanted & undesired
But it is mine....

Denied Reality

The is no agony greater than the
agony of desires unfulfilled
Unknown pleasures denied by brutal distance....

Fallen Apart

We all wear masks
I've worn mine so long I no longer
recognize the man beneath
Things fall apart...

Dominance-Submission-Sin

Lovers Light

I found my freedom bathed in my lovers light
Raw and unfiltered I have sought the
beast within A savage joy shared....

Role Reversal

Subdued innocence
As the wolf waits in the shadows
Little knowing the hunter has now become the prey
Roles reverse....

Claimed

With a firm hand he claimed her body
With a deep kiss he claimed her mind
Her heart his to protect and own....

Unmasked

The public mask I wear with polite acceptance
To drop all pretensions when alone with you
This is the real me
Yours....

Flawed Acceptance

Flawed, broken & deeply scarred
This man has captured her with his raw
acceptance of what he truly is
Unapologetic….

Bound Tight

Angel you have a body to chase the devil at night
Taking your faith from evenings twilight
To me you are bound tight….

Imaginations Release

By your hand & by my will you will
find the release you seek
Trembling as you are to imaginations purpose….

Provoked Readily

Strong hands consistently supportive of your needs
Assertive & knowing as required
Hard & unrelenting when provoked
You submit readily….

Friendship-Devotion-Solidarity

Ethereal Inspiration

My ethereal muse
Upon my knees I have pledged myself to you
Your happiness my reward, the gift of
your smile my inspiration….

Chained Dreams

Her heart's desire was chained to his dreams
Soaring high above in twilights embrace
She floats high among the clouds….

Bloodied Nightmares

Surrounding her weary warriors dreams
with white light, he finds a brief moments
respite from bloodied nightmares….

Remembered Pain

Doors designed to keep in remembered
pain thrown open
Held open by one whose grim determination
refuses to see you hurt….

Beastly Beauty

She has seen past the scars, held close to his brutal visage
What she knows of her beast is firmly
accepted and absolute....

Separating Illusion

Separation is an illusion
I have known your heart
Felt it's very beat as if it was my own
A sacred connection
Ours....

Precious Slumber

Sleep precious one, rest
Through fractured and constant pain, slumber
Where dreams are free from a reality all to short....

Wishful Touch

You lay in the dreaming moments
of sleep and drifting reality
Elusive as you are to my wishful touch
I have missed you....

Happiness-Joy-Rapture

Barred Solitude

There's light that guides my dreaming travels
This radiance my companion in barred solitude
Faith a known constant....

Cold Tranquillity

The tranquillity of the clouds forming in the long winter
There is a playful joy in the coldest of days....

Hopeful Faith

The righteous flight of a new day
Darkness fleeing from open horizons
Hope achieved with passionate faith....

Gifted Pathways

Auburn hair beauty silently focused
Her inner strength visible
A magical gift given to one who has lost his way....

Under Your Skin

In your blood & under your skin
Her presence alone brings about a persuasive weakness
A battle happily surrendered....

Clarified Chaos

In the midst of primal devastation
there is found raw beauty
Out of the chaos of life there is still clarity abound....

Redemption Found

The feminine form of divinity
Captured within a humble form
Flame haired and fiery winged
Redemption sought and found....

Losing Time

I have watched you with timeless intensity
Happily losing time in and around
your speechless beauty....

Love-Passion-Lust

Beautiful Temptation

His eyes reflect heavens stars, the passions light. Fiery red as desires flame is ignited with beauties tempting grace....

Devoted

You are loved
You are cherished
You are adored
And you are mine
This is what I feel
This is what I know....

Blind Touch

In shadows embrace she closes her eyes
A lover's caress known without sight
His touch leaving her breathless with need....

Committed Word

You are mine and I am yours
Nothing and no one can ever change that
This is my promise, this is my word, this is us....

Precious Intention

Your gentle moans the sweetest words never spoken
Breathless as you are to my loving intent
This time a precious memory....

Loving Protection

There are fewer vows more powerful than one made with whispered intensity, a man protects what he loves....

Northern Star

I don't want to count stars
The only one I care for is you, my north star
A lost man finding lost sleep in your dreams....

Peaceful Escape

In joy & sorrow, in your arms I'll find the peace I crave
Your deep kisses the escape I need from crushing reality...

Musing-Inspirational-Random

Fragile Promise

The most fragile things are found
to be the most determined
Grim fortitude holding to life's sweet promise....

Reckless

The best decisions ever made were
made with reckless abandon
To be lost within the moment is freedom true....

Empowering Choice

We all have the power to change our reality
Situations challenge our perceptions of control
What is within us, defines us....

Imperfectly Perfect

My greatest desire is for you to see yourself as I see you
All the more beautiful for your
wonderful imperfections....

Chaotic Static

Elusive shadows dance around words creation
Thoughtful static preventing writings cathartic relief
Frustrating….

Reapers Rejection

Whatever strength and whatever
grace I have I give to you
Even with the spectre of death looming
your radiance shines….

Pure Intent

There are fewer gifts more sacred than those given with selfless intent; unspoken gratitude is its own reward….

Soul Food

To live in a world with passionate restraint will leave the heart bereft and the soul malnourished….

Sadness-Loss-Grief

Closed Heart

Sought after darkness surrounds
Lost love found with weary vigilance
Always near but forever elusive....

Lonely Homestead

I have come to this most secret of places
A haven known by me and once known by you
This sanctuary empty without you....

Radiant Loss

This shadowed angelic warrior
Lifting the burden of lost light
A loss felt keenly with devastating knowledge of loss....

Solo Pairing

Walking through the fog
Steps fading with each movement I fade from myself,
I fade from you
We move on
Diminished....

Affection Lost

A cruel denial of what never was
The body blow felt with every heart beat
Time will not lessen this brutal longing….

Newly Broken

Heart break a hard memory
What was whole is now destroyed
The sense of bewildering abandonment
All consuming and raw….

Forsaken Grace

Chained, bound, fallen
The feral roar of soundless sorrow
Suffering savoured with rasping breath
Abandoned….

Risen Faith

Angels fall exposing radiant skin
She lies beneath a cloudy sky waiting
For a love that will make her soar again….

Wrath - Anger - Rage

Warring Peace

Darkness, rage, I burn so very hot if control is to slip
Focussed as I am on walking the way
of the peaceful warrior....

Vicious Lessons

Eternal vigilance, how can a warrior stand
down, surrender or retreat when this is
the only life he has ever known....

Untamed Hunting

In wild surrounds freedom is sought with tracked focus
Quarry, prey, meat
All the same to a hunter of the untamed....

Known Downfall

Her man & warrior lover
Surrounded by faithless enemies
He fights as he always has
Her heart breaks knowing he'll fall....

Hardened Pain

Visions of blood, visions of battle
The warriors rest, the soldiers respite
The quest lost, the trail cold
Heart hardened against known pain....

Upright Cleansing

Narrow vision seeking abhorrent evil
The gleaming blade prepared
Striking hard from a position of raging strength
A brutal cleansing ....

Presently Accepted

Present battles challenged
Once again alone & surrounded
Acceptance found with arms open
Unbowed the fight is joined....

Released Rage

You have no idea what your actions have released in me
This rage, this anger I thought long
buried for all eternity....

About the Author

RYAN BAIRD

Ryan Baird is a poet and wordsmith, using a combination of different poetic styles and themes. In this book you'll find primarily free verse poetry and micro poetry. As he has honed his writing skills he has branched out into other poetic styles which include, rhyming, acrostic and double acrostic poems covering a broad range of emotional musings. When he's not working as a Drill and Blast Trainer/Assessor on a faraway mine site in Australia, he can be found in his man cave at home seeking the cathartic release that only writing will give. He is currently writing several works, including a poetic collaboration with Sharon Johnson.

You can find him on Twitter at:
https://twitter.com/Pte_Ryan
or
Instagram at:
https://www.instagram.com/pte_ryan/